After Sex

Siofra Dromgoole

methuen | drama

LONDON • NEW YORK • OXFORD • NEW DELHI • SYDNEY

METHUEN DRAMA
Bloomsbury Publishing Plc
50 Bedford Square, London, WC1B 3DP, UK
1385 Broadway, New York, NY 10018, USA
29 Earlsfort Terrace, Dublin 2, Ireland

BLOOMSBURY, METHUEN DRAMA and the Methuen
Drama logo are trademarks of Bloomsbury Publishing Plc

First published in Great Britain 2024

Photography by Jake Bush and graphic design by Harry Warman

A catalogue record for this book is available from the British Library.

A catalog record for this book is available from the Library of Congress.

ISBN: PB: 978-1-3505-2579-5
ePDF: 978-1-3505-2580-1
eBook: 978-1-3505-2581-8

Series: Modern Plays

Typeset by Mark Heslington Ltd, Scarborough, North Yorkshire
Printed and bound in Great Britain

To find out more about our authors and books visit
www.bloomsbury.com and sign up for our newsletters.

Cast

HIM	Azan Ahmed
HER	Antonia Salib

Creative team

Writer	Siofra Dromgoole
Director/Producer	Izzy Parriss
Intimacy Director	Stella Moss
Associate Director	Philippa Lawford
Music and Sound Design	Helen Noir
Lighting Design	Simeon Miller
Set Consultant	Pip Terry
Movement Directors	Nadine Elise Muncey
	Rachel Laird
Movement Consultant	Stephanie Burrell
Stage Manager	James Christensen
PR	Chloé Nelkin Consulting
Marketing	Megan Gibbons

After Sex was a finalist for Platform Presents Prize in 2023. This production is the play's world premiere, produced by Izzy Parriss Productions and Three Sisters Productions in Association with the Arcola Theatre and supported using public funding by Arts Council England.

Thank you to all the generous supporters of *After Sex*, including Ed Cohen, Susie Parriss, Ripley Parker, Nick Drake, Aaron Martin, Rose Gardner, Steven and Linda Meadows, Grainne Dromgoole and David and Gill Wiggs.

HIM | Azan Ahmed

Azan most recently completed filming on the new BBC series We Go Again directed by Nathaniel Martello White, playing the role of Paul across four episodes. Next up, he'll be seen leading the world premiere of his own play, *Statues*, commissioned at The Bush in a co-production with Two Magpies, directed by Esme Allman.

Azan stars as series regular Eddie Suleman in the hugely popular ITV series *Van der Valk* alongside Marc Warren and most recently was seen in a guest role in ITVX's new comedy *Count Abdulla*. His further television credits include: *Mood* (BBC/Bonafide); *Hope Street* (BBC/Britbox); *Casualty* (BBC); and *Doctors* (BBC). Film roles include: *What's Love Got To Do With It?* (Instinct Productions) and *Now and Then* (BFI).

Most recently, he starred in the Omnibus production and tour of the powerful one-man show *10 Nights* by Shahid Iqbal Khan directed by Samir Bhamra. Before this, he was at the National Theatre playing the roles of Daulat and British Policeman in their stunning production of *The Father and the Assassin*. Azan played the role of Ferdinand in Shakespeare's Globe's latest production of *The Tempest*, directed by Diane Page. His other theatre credits include: *Conspiracy* (New Diorama Theatre and Underbelly Edinburgh); *This Isn't a True Story* (Almeida Theatre); *Cacophony* (Yard Theatre) and *Never Swim Alone* (Etcetera Theatre).

Azan is also an award- winning writer. His debut play *Daytime Deewane* (Half Moon and tour) won the 2023 Offie Award for Best TYA Writing. He is currently being mentored by Roy Williams as part of Hampstead Theatre's INSPIRE cohort.

Azan is the founder of Deen & Dunya, a platform for Muslim voices to be celebrated through poetry, music and performance – they have had enormous success to date selling out the Bush Theatre, Royal Court and The Globe.

HER | Antonia Salib

Antonia Salib is a British-Egyptian actor, director and workshop facilitator. She recently starred in *Hijack* (Apple TV+) opposite Idris Elba as well as appearing in Marvel's *Moon Knight* (Disney+) with Oscar Isaac and Ethan Hawke.

Her other acting credits include *The Play That Goes Wrong* (Duchess Theatre), *Black Ice* (Theatre503), *Biosphere* (Pleasance Theatre), *The Funeral* (King's Head Theatre) and *Know You Well* (Southwark Playhouse).

She has produced and starred in *Chronic*, a short film about chronic illness within a romantic relationship. For this, she was nominated for Best Actress at BIFA qualifying for the Little Wing Film Festival.

As a director she is currently developing a short film, *SEAMS*, and will be directing a sharing of new play, *Her Country* by Craig Henry. Previous directing credits include *SPY MOVIE: The Play!* (Hope Theatre) as assistant director, and *She is Taken Lightly* (Katzpace).

She is also an audition panel member for The Oxford School of Drama and has run workshops for Tonic Theatre.

Siofra Dromgoole | Writer

Siofra Dromgoole is an award-nominated playwright. Her plays, which include *Baby What Blessings* and *Walk Swiftly and With Purpose* have been performed to critical acclaim at theatres across the UK, London and Australia. She has screen projects in production and development, including with the BBC and Netflix. Her first book of poetry *Goodbye Scarecrow* was published by the San Mei Gallery, and she is co-artistic director of Three Sisters Productions.

Izzy Parriss | Director/Producer

Izzy Parriss is a freelance theatre director and producer.

She is the artistic director of Izzy Parriss Productions, lead producer and associate director at Tightrope Theatre and lead producer for The AIDS Plays Project.

Her freelance credits include work with Ambassador Theatre Group, Royal Central School of Speech and Drama, Theatre503, Three Sisters Productions, Omnibus Theatre, Theatr Clwyd, Yvonne Arnaud Theatre and Bomb Factory Theatre.

The production of *After Sex* by Siofra Dromgoole at the Arcola Theatre marks Izzy's London directorial debut.

Her associate directing credits include: *Ikaria* and *Cold Water*, both performed with Tightrope Theatre.

Stella Moss | Intimacy Director

Stella Moss is a London based critically acclaimed intimacy coordinator and director. Known for her work for both on stage and screen, Stella's approach to intimacy is defined as intuitive, authentic and collaborative, prioritising an inclusive representation of intimacy. Compassion, communication and humour is at the core of all of her work. Stella's international background and upbringing have shaped her understanding and interest in non-verbal communication and physical verbal cues, which continue to influence her work in creating nuanced portrayals of intimacy. Stella's background both as an award-winning producer, and previously as a performer, has informed how she navigates the role alongside each department and production. Her previous credits in intimacy coordination and direction include work in feature film, TV, music video and theatre with clients including Iconoclast, Lowkey Films, OB42, Pulse Films, Thimble Films, Tightrope Theatre, Goldsmiths University, Edge Hill University, MetFilm School and more.

Philippa Lawford | Associate Director

Philippa Lawford is a writer-director from London. Her debut play, *Ikaria*, won a runner-up award from the ATG Playwrights' Prize and an OFFIE Short Run Commendation, and was named no. 2 on Broadway World's list of Best Theatre of 2022. *Ikaria* toured the UK in 2023, culminating in an acclaimed run at the Park Theatre, where it was nominated for the Susan Smith Blackburn Prize. *Ikaria* was produced by Philippa's company, Tightrope Theatre, and was published by Methuen Drama. Philippa's second play, *Cold Water*, was staged at the Park Theatre in May 2024, and published by Methuen Drama.

Philippa also works as an assistant director and script reader/facilitator. She is a member of Marylebone Theatre's emerging writers group and has read for the Finborough and the ETPEP award. Philippa also co-runs Offshoots, a regular scratch night in London, and the Clonterbrook Arts Residency in Cheshire.

Helen Noir | Music and Sound Designer

Helen Noir is a London-based soprano who combines performance work with composing, orchestration, sound design and production, creating soundtracks for multiple film and theatre projects Helen is also resident composer of The AIDS Plays Project and a long-term member of cult performance art group Theo Adams Company.

Simeon Miller | Lighting Designer

Simeon has worked as a lighting designer since he graduated from Mountview Academy in 2010. He works across theatre, dance, musicals, 'gig theatre' and devised work. He enjoys contributing to new writing, especially socially and politically conscious work which amplifies oppressed and radical voices.

Selected recent credits include: *Brief Encounter* (Royal Exchange); *Silence* (UK tour); *Cowbois* (RSC and Royal Court); *Pass It On* (Bush

Theatre); *As We Face the Sun* (Bush Theatre); *Alice in Wonderland* (Liverpool Everyman and Plymouth Theatre Royal); *The Sun Shines for Everyone* (Lyric Hammersmith); *The Book of Will* (Queen's Theatre Hornchurch, Bolton Octagon and Shakespeare North Playhouse); *Ruckus* (Southwark Playhouse and Summerhall, Edinburgh); *Jekyll and Hyde* (Derby Theatre and Queen's Theatre Hornchurch); *Christmas in the Sunshine* (Unicorn Theatre); *Follow the Signs* (Soho Theatre); *The Poison Belt* (Jermyn Street Theatre); *Project Dictator* (New Diorama Theatre); *An Adventure* (Bolton Octagon); *Metamorphoses* (The Globe); *The Mob Reformers* (Lyric Hammersmith); *Subject Mater* (Edinburgh Fringe); *Black Holes* (international tour) and *High Rise eState of Mind* (UK tour).

His full portfolio and credits can be found online at *www.simeon. lighting*.

Pip Terry | Set Consultant

Pip Terry is a set and costume designer and scenic artist. She graduated from Wimbledon College of Art with a degree in Theatre Design in 2020. Pip won the Linbury Prize for Stage Design in 2021 and worked as the Kiln Theatre's resident assistant designer throughout 2022. She is currently designing *My English Persian Kitchen* (Traverse Theatre/Soho Theatre) and a schools tour of *The Shivers* with New Diorama Theatre.

Credits as assistant: *Ali The Musical* (Broadway); *Nachtland* (Young Vic); *A Christmas Carol* (Finnish National Opera); *Black Love, Girl on an Altar, The Darkest Part of the Night, Handbagged* (Kiln Theatre); *Kerry Jackson* (National Theatre).

Credits as Associate: *The Time Traveller's Wife* (Apollo Theatre); *Splintered* (Soho Theatre); *Pinocchio* (Unicorn Theatre); *The Tempest, Hamnet* (RSC); *Once On This Island* (Regent's Park Open Air Theatre).

Credits as designer: *Diva: Live From Hell* (Kings Head/Underbelly);*The Sex Ed Musical* (schools tour, Ice and Fire Theatre Company); *Playmaking Festival 2023* (RSC); *Rise* (Kiln Theatre, Young Company); *Sticks and Stones* (Tristan Bates); *The Hunting of the Snark, The House at the Centre of the World* (Rose Theatre, Youth Theatre); *Ad Nauseam* (Lyric Hammersmith's Evolution Festival).

Nadine Elise Muncey | Co-Movement Director

Nadine is a contemporary dance artist, choreographer and movement director.

Graduating from Trinity Laban Conservatoire of Music and Dance, she performed works by Joss Arnott, Hubert Essakow, Sonia Rafferty and Hofesh Shechter. She went on to study for an MA in Dance Performance, performing works by Karole Armitage, Marina Collard and Hetain Patel.

She has choreographed and performed *Surfacing, Resurfacing*, a site-specific work at John Maine's Arena, as well as co-creating and performing *Landscape No. 8* at Resolution Festival 2022. As part of Resolution 2023, she performed in *Gathering Clouds* by Petronella Wiehahn and premiered her own work titled *soft surge* – a contemporary dance work that she is continuing research for.

Nadine has performed works by Julian Nichols for Bodies in Action Dance, Extended Play and Róisıń Whelan Dance and has walked for fashion designer Izzy McCormac as part of her Jinal collection at Central Saint Martins. Nadine has also been involved in music videos for artists Cryalot, Rokia Kone, Henri, MAVICA and Dua Lipa.

Rachel Laird | Co-Movement Director

Rachel is a freelance dance artist from Scotland and trained at Copenhagen Contemporary Dance School for her postgraduate, Trinity Laban Conservatoire of Music and Dance for her BA (Hons) degree and prior to this at the Scottish School of Contemporary Dance and National Youth Dance Company of Scotland.

Since being freelance Rachel has performed for Highly Sprung, English National Opera, Garsington Opera, Peut-Être Theatre, Next Door Dance, Tess Letham, Roisin O'Brien, The Natashas Project, Page One Theatre and A Truefitt Collective among others. In 2019 she co-founded the dance theatre company Sliding Doors Collective.

Stephanie Burrell | Movement Consultant

Stephanie Burrell is an artist who works within dance and performance. Originally from Manchester, she trained at Trinity Laban Conservatoire of Music and Dance in Contemporary Dance before going onto study Spanish and German at King's College London.

Stephanie's performance credits span between London, Berlin and Mexico City.

Stephanie has performed for Hallomai Dance, West Green House Opera Festival and Ballhaus Naunynstraße in Berlin.

Her choreography work has seen her make and facilitate works for screen, stage and installation. Her credits include Freight Theatre, Phoebe Von Held Brecht installation at Raven Row and more recently music videos for Shivani Day and British Latin artist Sophie Castillo.

Stephanie also makes her own physical theatre work with collaborator Erin Hughes under Birthday Fish Theatre. 2024 will see their Edinburgh Fringe debut.

James Christensen | Stage Manager

James is a director, deviser, composer and stage manager from Melbourne, Australia. His work spans a range of styles including new writing, classical adaptation, experimental performance, musical, opera and live art – with a particular focus on formal innovation and collaborative interplay between varied artistic disciplines. He is currently the resident production manager for the Advanced Theatre Practice programme at Royal Central School of Speech and Drama.

Recent stage management credits include: *Othello* (Riverside Studios); Form(at) Festival (Camden People's Theatre); *Earthquakes in London* and *Nora: A Doll's House* (Rose Bruford College).

arcola
theatre

Arcola Theatre was founded by Mehmet Ergen and Leyla Nazli in September 2000. Originally located in a former textile factory on Arcola Street in Dalston, in January 2011 the theatre moved to its current location in a former paint-manufacturing workshop on Ashwin Street. In 2021, we opened an additional outdoor performance space just around the corner from the main building: Arcola Outside.

Arcola Theatre produces daring, high-quality theatre in the heart of East London. We commission and premiere exciting, original works alongside rare gems of world drama and bold new productions of classics. We work with creatives from across the globe, acting as a platform for emerging artists, providing them space to grow and explore, and similarly as a refuge for established artists refining their craft. Our socially engaged, international programme champions diversity, challenges the status quo, and stages trailblazing productions for everyone. Ticket prices are some of the most affordable in London, and we offer concessions for under 26s, senior citizens, those on disability benefits and unemployment benefits, as well as industry union members. We produce the yearly Grimeborn Opera Festival, hosting dozens of new and classical works from across the globe.

As part of our commitment to supporting the diversity of the theatre ecosystem, every year, we offer 26 weeks of free rehearsal space to culturally diverse and refugee artists; and our Participation department creates thousands of creative opportunities for the people of Hackney and beyond. Our pioneering environmental initiatives are award-winning and aim to make Arcola the world's first carbon-neutral theatre.

Arcola has won awards including the UK Theatre Award for Promotion of Diversity, The Stage Award for Sustainability and the Peter Brook Empty Space Award.

Acknowledgements

Thank you to my first readers and closest collaborators, Grainne and Cara. Thank you to my later readers, John Hoggarth and Tanya Ronder. Thank you to Clonterbrook Opera House and to Little Hatch residencies for the time and space to write better and dig deeper. Thank you to the Arts Council for supporting this production, and to Ed Cohen, Ripley Parker and Susie Parriss, for their generosity and belief in the project.

Thank you to my agent Jennie Miller, and to Rupert Stonehill and Jess Sykes; to Callan McCarthy and the team at Methuen; to Mehmet, Leyla, Imy, Millie and the team at the Arcola. Thank you to the brilliant creative team, and above all to Izzy Parriss, with whom it's been the greatest luck and joy to share the journey of this play.

For Ripley, who made this, and everything, possible

After Sex

*'What did you think, that joy
was some slight thing?'*

Mark Doty

Notes

The two characters should move between being expectant, elated, becoming – and being devastatingly cynical.

They are most scared of each other. They are most scared of themselves.

Both briefly believe the other holds the only possibility of hope.

There is nothing they don't say out loud, and yet everything remains unsaid. (That being true, words in brackets are probably unsaid.)

They wear their hearts on their sleeves: this is a secret.

Their hearts are already broken when it begins (The lake, still, before the stone has been skimmed, before the ripple, after the last one) But they are allowed to forget this.

Lighting and sound design should be excellent.

Before the play begins Polly and Isaac, or Niamh and Isiah, or Charlie and Ishmael, or whatever they are called, know each other through work.

They have EVERYTHING, but NOTHING in common.

Dashes (–) indicate a character breaking off.

Ellipses (. . .) indicate a character trailing off.

Slashes (/) indicate where one is interrupted by another.

Scene One. 'I Have An Other-ache'

Two people lie near each other, post-coital. She is on her phone. She goes to show him something.

Her   My friend just sent me this.

It's funny because she's a sag and I don't have a lot of sag energy in my life, probably for this exact reason.

You're not a horoscope guy, are you. Kay, ignore.

A pause.

Him   Did you . . .

Her   No. It felt great, but no.

Him   I have an idea.

Her   Yes.

Him   Why don't you sit on my face and tell me about my star sign and see how long you can keep talking for.

Her   Okay.

She gets into position.

I'll do you a birth chart. When were you born?

Him   Third October.

Her   What year?

Him   1993.

Her   Where were you born?

Him   Whitby.

Her   And is ( ) short for ( )?

Him   Yeah.

Her   Okay, so right about now someone is harvesting your data.

He takes a new grip on her thighs. We should feel that either could swing the other round the room at any point. (This is not because one or the other needs to be slim or athletic, but because they have a strong physical connection.)

Him   Is this okay?

A muffled noise of approval. She looks into the distance. She looks slightly uncomfortable. She loses track of her thought.

Her (*to audience*)   I always end up wondering if people know that what I'm getting off on has nothing to do with them. Because what I'm actually thinking about – it's how does right here right now my flesh look slapping against itself. It's did he think I would look like this and does he still like me, it's what do I look like compared to the last person he saw naked and did I remember to send the email that I need to have sent by tomorrow. It's how to – how to not – it's wanting to prise open his mouth with my finger and floss his teeth with my tongue, it's the kisses earlier that counted for more than the sex does now, all the kinds, fluttering, and it's have I brushed my own teeth and should I close my eyes and do I like him and does he like me and will I have a child one day – and then, then here it is the slopes of pleasure that are both inside and outside of myself and I want and don't want it, all the sparrows, all of the special providence falling – because it's rainbows undone and the opaque poetry of other people and it all floats up across the grossness of the bodies, wet and dry and plunging and I feel bad because it's not about the person and then it's all about the person and there are times when it's metaphysical and times when it just isn't and sometimes they're inside me and I want to say, if you were just a little less hard I could probably come, I want to say, what are you thinking about right now, I want to say are you thinking about me, and then the aches and pains and the soreness that is cleansing, the lagoon of you or the moon of me – what I'd really like to do is spend an evening picking dirt out from under your toenails and tearing the dead skin off your feet.

She orgasms. They roll apart. Maybe he gets out his phone.

Her   I mean it makes sense you're definitely an air sign.

Him   Why?

Her   I tend to gravitate toward air signs.

No but seriously, because you're very mercurial but you seem to consider each mood you have as absolutely permanent.

Him   Do you think I have a lot of moods.

Her   Yes.

She worries this was too personal.

Sorry.

Him   Why sorry? You don't need to be sorry.

Scene Two. In Which They Think About Telling Each Other Things

The same couple. Post-coital, in a different position.

Him   Favourite food.

Her   Yeah?

Him   What would you eat on death row?

Her   Steak, rare steak, with potatoes swimming in cream.

Him   No vegetables?

Her   No, but a chocolate fondant for pudding. Morning sex?

Him   Ambivalent, but I can't stand kissing.

Her   Kissing in the morning is atrocious.

Him   What's the last book you read?

Her   *Epistemology of the Closet* by Eve Sedgwick. Pets?

Him   Weird.

Her   Right? For people who aren't able to deal with emotionally complex needs.

Him   We had a dog growing up and I loved him.

Her   We had guinea pigs and they all died. We kept them outside in a hutch and they kept freezing to death, and we'd find them in the morning, like stiff little blankets right outside the kitchen door, where they'd been trying to get back in.

Him   The dog was ill for a long time, and one day my mum took him out into the field and I heard a shot, just one. And I remember dinner that night with me and my sister sobbing and Mum not saying a word, just sitting there.

Her   We flushed goldfish down the toilet.

Him   But when I asked her about it recently she said I was mad, that she'd taken the dog into a vet to be put down. That I'd made the whole thing up.

Beat.

Her   What's your favourite mood?

Him   I think that's quite an emotionally privileged question to ask

Her   What?

Him   You have clearly never been on anti-depressants.

Her   Poor darling. How many times a week do you shower?

Him   Every day.

Her   Max three times.

Him   How many times a day do you brush your teeth?

Her   Two!

Him   Good.

Her   Can you cook?

Him   Can you clean?

Her   Do you drive?

Him   Yes.

Her   I can't. And I think I can clean but apparently my flatmates say I don't see dirt in the way other people do, like my baseline of cleanliness might be different from yours. What do you think about Tony Blair?

Him   War criminal.

Her   Hot.

Him   What do your parents think about Tony Blair?

Her   Cool Britannia. Disillusionment. Etc. Did you go to private school?

Him   No.

Her   Would you send your kids to private school?

Him   No.

Her   Obviously if I had my way, I'd have all private schools abolished but . . .

Him   But . . .

Her   But also in the meantime like obviously I'm going to want the best for my kids, it's like also does nepotism always have to be the worst thing in the world like, why is it such a dirty word?

Him   Fuck.

Her   Yeah?

Him   I'm out.

Her   Favourite line of poetry?

Pause.

Him   'I am not yet born, provide me / with water to dandle me, grass to grow for me, trees to talk / to me, sky to sing to me, birds and a white light / at the back of my mind to guide me.'

Pause.

Her   What's your favourite part of your body?

Him   Shoulders. What's your favourite part of my body?

Her   Shoulders. Mine?

Him   Stomach.

Her   Feet. What do you find sexiest?

Him   I find stretch marks sexy.

Her   Cellulite?

Him   I find cellulite sexy.

Her   I find beer bellies sexy.

Him   I find bunions sexy.

Her   I find sloping shoulders and a slight stoop sexy.

Him   You know what, I just like bodies. Bodies are beautiful.

Her   That's what you're meant to say.

Him   It's true though. Bodies are what make bodies beautiful.

Her   What's your favourite food?

Him   Chicken on thickly buttered bread.

Her   '(I do not know what it is about you that closes / and opens / only something in me understands / the voice of your eyes is deeper than all roses) / nobody, not even the rain, has such small hands.' My favourite line of poetry, you can't hear but there are brackets from the first line until the first roses.

He says her name, perhaps with a question mark.

What?

Him   Nothing.

Scene Three. In Which They Decide Not To Tell Each Other Things

They are having sex. If this is being portrayed literally (and it does not have to be portrayed literally) he is on top, with her legs over his shoulders.

Her   Baby, I want you to come, I want you to come inside of me baby, I want to feel you come.

He stops.

Him   You don't need to cheerlead me.

Her   I know.

Him   I don't need –

Her   I just want you to come, what's wrong with that?

Him   It's just – it's actually a lot of pressure, it doesn't actually help me.

Her   Sorry.

Beat.

Him   It makes me feel like you just want it over with. Or like we're just using each others genitals for our own masturbation, does that make sense?

Her   It does actually. Thank you for saying.

They lie for a little. Maybe tracing each others bodies.

Him   Are we going to tell people?

Her   What do you mean?

Him   Are we going to tell people at work.

Her   I don't want to. Is that okay?

It's just imagining – I don't know – Magda watching me en route to the photocopier and thinking, is she limping like that because they spent the night fucking doggy-style, like on a carpet, and they rubbed all the skin off her knees.

Him   Really?

Her   No. It's. More like, what would we say, like what is there to say.

Him   Are you asking me to define what we're doing here?

Her   No.

I'm not.

Him   Hard to be like, yeah, we're fucking.

And last week you came seven times.

Her   Five.

Him   You said seven. I mean, obviously I'll accept your number.

Pause.

Her   You know, this is actually the first time I've done this.

Him   What do you mean?

Her   Slept with someone casually.

Him   Yeah?

Her   Had repeated casual sex.

Him   That sounds quite clinical.

Her   I'm actually kind of proud.

Him   That's good. It's probably all I'm good for at the moment.

Her   Why?

Him   Well, I'm just – I guess not in a relationship place.

Her   And we work together.

Him   Yeah, you're technically my boss.

Her   I'm not – argh.

Him   What?

Her   I can't help it. The Disney in me immediately sees those things as obstacles that will be overcome by the strength of our eventual love.

I'm joking.

Do you use apps?

Him   The thing about dating apps is that they don't want you to be in a longterm relationship. Not really. Cui bono, right?

Her   It's really sexy when you explain things to me.

Him   They want you to keep using them – so the best possible outcome is that you have a few short-term flings. Enough to think that the app is working, but that the problem is you.

Her   So you use apps because you *don't* want to be in a relationship?

Him   Exactly.

Her   And you don't want to be in a relationship because . . .

I'm not suggesting. I'm not saying that's what would happen to us, or even that that's what I want, I'm just interested.

Him   Interested.

Her   Yes. In you. If we're going to do this – this *casual* thing. I think. I think I need to know you a bit better.

Him   Okay. So, ask. Anything you like.

A long-ish and studied pause.

Her   If you had to fuck a Disney princess, which would it be? Animals included.

Scene Four. In Which They Tell Each Other All The Things

They have just finished having sex. He is wrapping the condom up.

Her   There is literally nothing more depressing than a condom post sex. Remembering I basically had a bin-bag right up inside me the entire time.

Him   Um, okay.

Her   I'm not insulting *you*, just *it*. Not exactly high romance.

Him   We don't have much of a choice.

Her   Well, I'm on the pill.

I did have a coil /

Him   What kind?

Her   Copper. I ended up getting ill once a month. When I took it out I was going to get a hormonal one but then I wasn't sure . . .

Him   Wasn't sure?

Her   Don't freak out. This isn't relevant to 'us' you / and I

Him   Okay /

Her   But I realised I'd probably want kids in the next five years, so it didn't seem worth it. To get all cranked open etc etc.

Him   Makes sense.

Her   But that's not the point, what I meant to say is that I'm on the pill so I can't get pregnant and we don't actually have to use condoms.

Him   I don't know if that's a good idea.

Her   Because?

Him   Because the other reasons people use condoms. I don't know who else you're sleeping with. You don't know –

Her   Right. Yeah.

Brief pause.

I kissed someone last night actually.

Him   That's nice.

Her   I went to a party and I didn't really know anyone there and it seemed the easiest way to have a good time.

Him   I get that.

Her   Are you jealous?

Him   No.

Her   Why aren't you jealous.

Him   I don't know.

Her (*playful*)   I want you to want me enough that you don't want [me] to be with anyone else.

Him   I don't think that's how my kind of want works.

Pause, where they are occupied. Maybe they are now clothed and making the bed they had left in disarray. Or they are building something, or painting a wall.

Her   Would you like to try anal?

Him   Sure. Do you want to?

Her   Not really.

Brief pause.

I think the problem is that you don't really know what you want.

Him   We don't have to do this.

Her   What do you mean?

Him   Like, we could make a decision just to not do this? If we're just two people who like each other, and have really good sex.

Her   Are we just two people who like each other and have really good sex?

Him   I care about you.

Her   Great.

Him   And I genuinely respect you.

Her   Sexy.

Him   Well.

Her (*not quite playful*)   Sometimes I think I am just All Women to you.

Him   What do you mean?

Her   No you. Explain what you mean. About the decision.

Him   Like, if we could find a way to be with each other, totally, but without the trying to define it. Without making it more difficult. Doing all the awful things people do in relationships – you know. Re-aligning their happinesses. Making compromises, and pretending the result is something they both wanted. Raking over past traumas, so they can place them side by side.

Her   'You fall in love, only to realise you are at the mercy of someone else's childhood.'

Him   What?

Her   Nothing. Sorry. No, I get it. I don't need to know what happened to you at four, when your pet mouse died and you kept its body. And then days later found it covered in maggots and suddenly understood Death and Life and Decay.

Him   Or at seven, when you were hiding under the table, and saw your mum's feet tucked around another man's legs

Her   Or twelve, when you put your head beneath a cider tap and drank so much that you fell over in the dirt outside the pub, and couldn't get up, just lay there for hours.

Him   I don't need to know the first time you kissed someone.

Her   Or when you spied on your aunt's thighs under the table.

Him   Yeah, I won't tell you about Maggie, my cousin, who asked me to show her my penis.

Her   I won't tell you about how when I lost my virginity I was so ashamed that I lied about it, and the man thought he was going mad.

Him   Gaslighting.

She raises an eyebrow.

I won't tell you about how I was never close to my dad. How he left us when I was four years old, and broke my mum's heart. How she never got over it.

Her   How I stole money from my parents.

Him   The time I read my aunt's texts, the aunt with the thighs.

Her   My affair with my teacher.

Him   My eating disorder.

Her   My binge drinking.

A pause. They are holding hands.

Her   But if. If we don't. If we don't tell those things are we anything to each other at all.

Him   If we don't tell each other those things, I could be anyone. You could be anyone.

Scene Five. In Which She Tries Not To Be Excited

On the phone to her sister. She is not someone who can stay still on the phone.

Her   Tall. Funny.

I don't really know. Like, he's not the strong silent type.

No, hundred per cent not a lad. / I actually think he doesn't fit a single stereotype?

No, I am not in love.

From work actually. We're not telling anyone.

Yeah, I guess it doesn't sound.

But it's actually.

Healthy?

I don't know. Very boundaries anyway.

I don't think that is actually therapy speak I think it means something very specific which it's possible to implement in life.

Okay fine, but it's not 'therapy speak' with those weighted quotation marks.

I *am* charming – you just don't bring it out in me. How are you?

Yeah, my friend Magda goes there, I think it's discounted through the office. But it's v. gym bunnies, green juice for ten pounds plus vibes. How can you afford that?

B, I love you but I can't lend you money to waste on that.

Her sister says something that makes her laugh.

No, I don't think that intimacy has been ruined by capitalism you –

Yeah okay, that does track.

No label and that's okay, I'm just not ready. My jealousy is on steroids.

Nu uh, way too soon. You try walking in on your boyfriend and his best [friend] –

Right. I'm scared that if I feel even one thing it'll open all the rest of it up. Right now I don't have to worry about whether I'm enough because I'm not even his.

No, not in a gendered way, like he's not mine either.

I don't know, whatever. Cycles of trauma.

B, I can lend you money but you will need to pay it back? Okay. Like by the end of the month kind of time?

She smiles.

Yeah. And I'll see you Sunday? *Don't* say prosexy that's so cringe.

I'll send the money now. I love you.

Scene Six. In Which She Works Through Things

Him   Okay, so the game is, one of us says something, and the other has to guess whether it's a fetish or a phobia.

Her   Um. Spanking. Choking. Bdsm.

Him   Sure or /

Her   Twins /

Him   More inventive.

Her   What, like octopi?

Him   That's actually a really respected porn genre.

Her   Okay, like being baked into a cake. Or being rolled up in dough and flying round the moon, and it slapping against you, all peaty. Or if you were rolled in mud or if like cannibals had you in a pot.

Him   Or like church bells pealing against a midsummer sky.

Her   Or like having several wives and gout? Okay.

A pause.

Him   I can go first.

Her   Okay, no, I have one.

Him   Yes.

Her   So you have a best friend.

Him   Yes.

Her   Let's say the best friend's called Leo.

Him   Okay.

Her   And you've always fancied the friend, but you're both straight.

Him   I'm not straight, I'm bisexual.

Her   In this fantasy you're straight.

Him   I don't know how I feel about that, it's a bit erasing.

Her   It's my fantasy.

Him   It's my identity.

I'm joking, I want to hear.

Her   Okay, and you've both always fancied each other, but you can't have sex.

Him   Because?

Her   Because you're both straight. And you're going out with me and you fancy me and we like (*she is not very good at swearing*) fucking but whenever I'm with the two of you I can see there's something there. And maybe the friend, Leo, he really resents me but he also looks at me too long, his gaze lingers on me and my body feels like a light, bright thing with all this from both of you being chanelled at it.

Maybe they are both masturbating. This doesn't have to be represented literally.

And one day it's the morning and we wake up, a little bit hungover. I don't want to have sex because I haven't brushed my teeth yet, but I start giving you head. And Leo comes in without knocking, and rather than leaving straight away he leers, a bit unpleasantly. I don't stop giving you head, and you look at me and I consent with my eyes and you tell him he doesn't need to leave, that he can stay if he likes.

Maybe they are touching each other.

And so he starts having a conversation – about I don't know, where the big pot is or where the bin liners are and then talking about the day and what you're going to do together and all the while he's watching me and watching you and I can see he has an erection. And I make a motion and it's clear what I'm saying. He comes and stands behind me, running his hands over me and I make it okay, I make it okay that he moves inside of me, and when you both groan at the same time, I know it's that you're watching each other, looking straight into each others eyes. Is this weird?

Him   No.

Maybe she is looking at him.

Her   It's important that it's morning, the most important thing about it all is that it's morning and the sun is starting to stream in, and we're a little bit crusty and crinkly and hungover, and my pubic hair is matted with your sperm from the night before. Thanks for not making that weird.

Scene Seven. In Which They Take Leaps And Bounds

They are at a club with friends from work. They are leaving the toilet and hastily rearranging their clothes as they make their way to the bar to order drinks. It's hard to hear each other over the noise. They are hanging from each other's bodies.

Her   Do you think they've guessed?

Him   What?

Her   Do you think they know we're together?

Him   Yeah. I think. Probably, yeah.

Her   I don't think I mind

Him   What?

Her   Do you mind?

He smiles.

Him (*to bartender*)   Two double vodka sodas, please.

(*To* **Her**.) I've never done that before.

Her   That? Oh that. Oh.

Him   You have, haven't you.

Her   Ohmygod. You're jealous.

Him   I'm not –

Her   Shhh. Please don't spoil this for me. You're jealous.

They both wave their credit cards to pay.

Him   No, I'll –

Her   Let me.

Him   I want to. (*suggestive*) You can . . . (*drops the act*) You can promise to come home with me and stay tomorrow when I'm hungover, and put your hand across my forehead while we watch TV.

They might kiss. They go to dance.

They move to their own rhythms for a little bit, at first awkward, but then they get it.

The music shifts and they move toward each other, dancing seriously, and then grinding against each other, sweaty and ecstatic. They leave the club, high as kites.

Her   That was –

Him   I feel –

Her   On top of the world I –

Him   Crispy bright new earth new world –

Her   Everything is new and –

Him   Everything is us?

Her   Your laugh sounds different.

Him   What do you mean?

Her   You have a different laugh, it's like I can hear the gravel in it but also I can hear it high pitched. It's like so many pitches, tolling mid-morning summer bells.

They have arrived home. They are still high. They lie on the floor.

Her   This is my special stone. I found it on a beach in Yorkshire and someone told me it wasn't a stone, it was smog.

Him   Smog?

Her   Sorry, smelt – like bits of waste from a factory that have washed into the sea and then folded over time, not crystallised I guess but somehow compacted into what is now this rock. You can see it's kind of porous and it's all of these different colours.

A pause. He moves the stone to her belly.

Him   What if it wasn't a stone?

Her   What?

Him   Look, like this. What if it's wasn't a stone, what if it's a baby, what if this was our baby.

They both stroke it.

Her   Is it okay that that turns me on?

Him   It turns me on.

Her   I'm just worried because I think what I'm being turned on by is the fact that you're imagining a stable future with me whereas what you're being turned on by is the potential potency of your own sperm.

Him   Do you always have to say everything you mean?

Pause.

Her   Can you tell me something nice?

Him   What do you mean?

Her   Something soft and nice that I can hold on to tomorrow. Or on Monday, when we go back into the office and everyone raises their eyes and asks questions and I don't have any real answers to give them.

Anything.

Him   I think you'd be beautiful with a pregnant belly.

Her   You're high.

Him   No, really.

I'm not good with labels –

Her   I didn't ask for / a

Him   and I don't know if I –

Or what I . . .

Her   Expected?

Him   Yeah sure, expected.

Not this anyway.

I feel

Her   Yeah?

Him   Like a lot.

Her (*laughing, slightly mocking*)   Like a lot.

Him   Yeah.

Her   Like a lot a lot?

Him   Yeah.

Her   Like a huge amount?

Him   Sure.

Her   Like hundreds and thousands?

Him   Maybe.

Her   Like hundreds of thousands of millions?

Him (*firmly*)   Like a lot.

They hold each other.

And also

Her   Yeah?

Him   Kind of

Peaceful.

Scene Eight. In Which He Works Through Things

Him   Stand there. Take off your jumper.

I'm trying something.

Her   Okay.

Him   Take off your tights. Take off your pants. Touch yourself.

They look into each other's eyes.

Okay, you go. Fetish or phobia.

Her   It's your turn.

Him   Okay. Imagine I'm just doing like

Him   Like

Him   Like yoga.

Her   Do you do –

Him   No, not the point. And we live together. And you're in the other room. And you're working. And I'm doing yoga. That's it.

Her   That's it?

Him   Yeah, that's it.

No, maybe you come into the room to ask me a question about – about where the big pot is or where the bin liners are – but you see that I'm in supta baddha konasana, so you don't ask but you watch me for like two seconds in a kind of calm slightly proprietorial way, and then you walk out again and go back to writing, and I never know what you came in for. Or maybe as you leave I ask you what you want and you say don't worry and I say okay and it's slightly passive aggressive but that's fine, because we say so many things to each other that not every single one has to be weighty or meaningful anymore.

Her   Phobia?

Him   Right.

They both know it's a fetish.

Scene Nine. In Which They Are Unsure

They take off all of their clothes. They have sex.

Him   Sometimes I think you're pandering to my ego.

Her   That's because sometimes I'm pandering to your ego.

They put each other's clothes back on.

Scene Ten. In Which He Has An Opportunity He Does Not Take

They are in the same room. Foreplay. Possibly dancing their first dance as they say the following words. Grinning, though not sure what they're mocking.

Her   Sometimes I am a Radical Feminist but sometimes I think Girls Just Wanna Have Fun.

Him   I don't know if those are mutually exclusive concepts.

Her   Sometimes I think I'm polyamorous, and sometimes I am all about the industrial marriage complex.

Him   Okay?

Her   Like all I want is to be on that box-set death-march straight person pipeline.

Him   Polyamory is an orientation.

Her   Is it though? Or do you just want to sleep with multiple people because you're afraid of commitment because that's. Not the same thing.

Him   I get the allure though.

Her   Of /

Him   Of settling down. Of having a definitive role to play. Like if I was someone who was en route, and I had a whole obvious path in front of me and a set of answers for when people asked me, How Are You and Do You Have a Girlfriend and What's the Timeline.

Her   Seriously?

Him   And best of all – if I had a baby. If I had a baby and then there was something else to do all the things for, there was a reason that was not just me, and I wouldn't even be playing a role any more because I wouldn't have the time to think about it, it would be nappies and gooey food, and is this the right temperature bath.

Her   But that's probably not a good reason to settle down.

Him   Right.

His phone rings. They stop dancing, interrupted.

Him   Is it okay if I

Her   Of course, of course.

He was maybe expecting her to leave to let him make the call, but instead she busies herself, and listens whilst pretending not to.

Him   Hi, Mum.

I did, I texted you.

I would never have ignored a call.

Sorry, I must have missed it.

Of course I do, she used to come and look after us when –

Yes, I remember, her daughter was the same age as –

I don't think I ever wore a Snow White dress, I think I'd remember that.

She's – fuck.

I'm so sorry. How did you?

But you're okay?

Of course, I'll reach out, I'll message her on

Yeah no. Maybe.

Of course. I miss you too.

Soon, I promise.

It's only a week and a half.

No, I can't do

I can't –

Next weekend then.

He grows self-conscious, acts as if she can't hear.

No, I'd tell you if there was anyone.

Yeah.

Love you too.

Scene Eleven. In Which They Are Not Fighting

They sit, fairly far from each other, on their phones. They smile at each other, holding the gaze.

He breaks it and types. She starts typing quicker.

He pauses. She pauses.

He starts typing again, she starts typing again.

Another brief pause.

Him   Want to watch something?

Her   Yeah. Yeah. I've just got to reply to this. Life admin.

She taps and types furiously, emptily.

Finally.

Yawns. Goes to sit near him.

Her   This is nice, isn't it.

Him   Yeah.

Her   I'm glad we can be bored together now, you know. At first it was like AH I NEED TO BE INTERESTING ALL THE TIME.

She waits for him to tell her she is interesting all the time. He doesn't.

How's your mum?

Him   She's good.

Her   When did you last see her?

Him   Two weeks ago.

A pause. He is trying to offer her something.

I used to go down to see her almost once a week. But I'm trying to.

Her   I get it. It's hard to work out what the appropriate distance is with family. Like how to be there for them without losing yourself. Or how to have your own expectations for yourself, rather than their expectations for you.

Him   Not really. She brought me up alone. And now my sister lives in Australia, and sometimes I think she has no one and the least I could do is visit her.

Her   I didn't know that.

Him   Like how hard is it for her only son to take the time to go down and visit her.

Her   You have a whole life. Work, and friends – and it can take a lot to –

Him   I know you're trying to be helpful, but I didn't ask for [advice].

Shall we watch something?

Her   Why are you avoiding this conversation?

Him   This isn't a conversation, I don't have anything to say about my mum. She's well, and I'm going to see her soon. What would you like to watch?

Her   I don't want to watch anything, I want to talk.

A pause.

How often do you think about your genitals?

Him   I don't know.

Her   I think it would make such a difference if I could pee standing up. Like literally all the difference in the world.

Him   That's pretty essentialist of you actually.

I feel like every time we fight you find a way to bring up the fact I'm a man and you're a woman.

Her   We're not fighting.

Scene Twelve. In Which They Make Up

They are having sex in the dark. It sounds a little angry. She starts to cry. He turns on a light.

Him   Hey. Hey. What's wrong? Shh, what's wrong?

Her   I just don't think we have very much in common.

Him   We literally – we work in the same office. We live in the same city. We both had pets. We both really like steak.

Her   But they're not the important things. I feel like we confused small things with big ones.

Him   Is there anything I can do to make you feel better?

Her   Will you tell me something?

Him   Tell you what?

Her   I don't know, just something.

Him   Like when Magda threw a glass of wine over our boss on her first day of work?

She laughs. Her sobs are more watery now.

Her   No, more like. Something you're scared of.

Him   I'm scared of being looked after.

Her   Do you know why?

Him   I'm scared that if I let someone look after me, I'll need them, and then they'll go away. No, that's not quite right.

I'm scared that if I let someone look after me, I'll break them. That if they really see what's at the heart of me, they'll break into a million tiny little pieces and I'll get even more lost trying to put those pieces back together. That if they see how much pain I'm in I'll have to acknowledge it, and then we'll never get out of bed again.

What about you?

Her   I'm scared that I'm boring. And that if I let someone in, that's what they'll find out.

Him   I like boring.

Scene Thirteen. In Which She Shows She Has Been Listening

Her   Okay, what if we were on a desert island.

Him   Yes.

Her   We're the only two people on a desert island. We've been shipwrecked.

Him   Or

Her   Yes?

Him   I've been shipwrecked. And it's your desert island

Her   Why was I there?

Him   You were exiled. And I wash up on your shore, and you're suspicious. And you tie me to a palm tree by my ankle, and twine my wrists together. You come and talk to me every day, and you feed me yourself. You fill coconut shells with water, and raise them to my lips and I sip slowly.

Her   Do we fall in love?

Him   We get to know each other, slowly. And then –

Her   Bandits.

Him   Really?

Her   Pirates!

Him   I'm not sure.

Her   Tightrope walkers.

Him   What are tightrope walkers doing –

Her   They're swinging from tree to tree. They're coming closer to us. We run.

Him   I'm tied up.

Her   You're right, it's too late to run. And they're probably cannibals.

Him (*resigning*)   They're definitely cannibals.

Her   And they're going to cook you and eat you and roast you and stew you.

Him   I think it's important that when we do this we make sure we're having the same fantasy.

During this next, he at first thinks she hasn't listened to him, but she has.

Her   I try to untie your wrists, but I did the knots too well, and even I can't untangle them. So I stand my ground. I gather all my courage and I stand in front of you and as the tightrope-walking cannibals approach I tell them you're mine. There are dozens of them, armed with streamers and batons and flame-throwers, one wearing pink tights and another with a ringmaster's top hat. And then just me. But something in my stance means they know they've lost. They can't have you. You are mine to feed and water and look after. And when I roar they turn around and disappear into the waves.

Him   Underwater tightrope-walkers.

Her   And the desert island is ours again. And I ask you if you want me to untie you.

Him   And I say no. Thank you, but no.

Scene Fourteen. In Which They Briefly Believe There Is Nothing In The World Which Could Separate Them

They dance. It's probably some kind of a tango.

Briefly, they believe in forever.

The dance is interrupted.

Scene Fifteen. In Which 'Forever' Is Immediately Tested

Her   What would you think if my period was late?

Him   You.

Her   Ten days late.

Him   Okay.

Her   The world is coming to an end. You can't have a child when you know they're going to live to see the world end.

Him   No.

Her   I couldn't birth a baby into a world in which I have only really enjoyed thirty per cent of my time.

Him   Yes.

Her   And even if they don't suffer, even if they managed to avoid all of our depressive genes. There'll be a decision that is part of making the rest of the world suffer whilst they stay fine in the West or the Global North or whatever we're calling it now.

I can barely even boil eggs.

Him   I can cook.

Her   And those problems with shifting baselines of cleanliness.

Him   I can clean.

Her   And we don't really. We don't really know each other. I don't really even know what you feel about me, bar the fact we have good sex. We haven't said the big words.

He looks at her.

I'm scared.

Him   Nobody's perfect.

Scene Sixteen. In Which They Briefly Believe There Is Nothing In The World Which Could Separate Them (Part ii)

They continue their dance.

It's probably now some kind of a waltz.

There is a timid fluency.

Scene Seventeen. In Which It Could, But Doesn't

They sit together. She is draining the last of a huge bottle of water. There are another two beside her. She takes out a pregnancy test.

Her   Okay.

Him   Okay.

Her   You know this is so unlikely? And if it's not, I'm sorry I've made such a fuss. It's really weird of me actually. Sorry.

Him   It's not weird.

Her   Sorry, I don't mean to self-flagellate.

Him   You don't need to be sorry.

Her   And I need you to know.

Him   Yes?

Her   I know we were joking last night. I know that's not how you really feel.

Him   You don't

Let's just find out, okay? And make all the decisions from there.

Her   Okay. You know.

I love you.

This is the first time they've said this. She goes quickly into the bathroom, not leaving the chance for him to say anything. Although he could have said something.

Him (*to the audience*)   This moment. This moment where a huge IF is over us, where everything is possible. Where two opposite things can co-exist. A kind of quantum grammar where she could be pregnant, or not.

Do I love her? Does it matter? I used to say it to my mother every other moment of the day. I love you if she got up, I love you if she didn't. I love you as a well done if she managed to eat, I love you to reassure when if she didn't. As if it could kind of stopper up all the desperate need she – But I guess it was a bit like putting a pebble in front of the mouth of a cave. Just a phrase. I love you to say sorry I love you to say I'm here, I love you to say please don't hate me, please like me, please want me.

And I'm broken and she's broken and we just want a child so that we don't have to look at our own brokenness any more. We want to get away from –

But oh, imagine it – foetus, little strawberry, melon ball, watermelon, one day eyes opening. Collection of cells that could go on to hold both of us, could go on to be the entire world or live a tiny life but still be the whole of our world. And we would always be bound to each other through what it was to care for a human and maybe the mistake we made would turn into the greatest thing either of us would ever could ever do.

And maybe. Maybe I do want her. And maybe this baby would tie me to her, when she finds out about how my hands sometimes smell like onions in the morning. Or how long my front teeth are, or how I repeat the same set of four to five jokes whenever I meet someone new, or how I don't have much ambition, not really, I only want to have enough money to buy clothes that allow me to fit in, I only want to have a child who each morning I can say I love you to as they get up, brush their teeth, put on their clothes and go to school, I –

She comes out of the toilet. She's holding the stick. A long pause.

Her   I'm pregnant.

He looks to her for an inclination of how she's feeling. She shakes her head.

Him (*to audience*)   Quantum grammar. When sometimes things end before they begin.

Scene Eighteen. Limbo

Her   Tell me about your dreams.

Him   My dreams.

Her   Yes.

Him   I dreamt of birds last night.

There were spirals everywhere, these whorls growing larger and larger.

What about yours?

Her   I dreamt I was taking off my clothes in front of someone without a face, and I felt so scared. Like I was admitting something. I don't know what – like I had a new kind of body that I didn't recognise. And taking off each item took so much bravery.

Him   What were you scared of?

Her   I don't know. The faceless person not loving me? Not finding me attractive? Realising I didn't love them or find them attractive?

Him   Was I the faceless person?

Her   Honestly, I don't know.

We can't have a baby just because.

Him   I didn't say –

Her   Okay. Okay. What if you're a doctor, and I'm a nurse

Him   Can we swap that round, that feels seedy.

Her   Okay, I'm the patient.

Come on.

Him   What's wrong with you?

Her   My head hurts.

Him   I can fix that.

Does that help?

Her   Yes. But now there's another part of me that hurts.

Him   Here?

Her   No

Him   Here?

She nods.

Him   Closer? Closer?

Her   Yes, just there that's – that's – that's.

She holds his hand, stops the movement.

Imagine if I was like, my heart hurts

Him   Yeah /

Her   And you replied, I can fix that.

Him   I don't know.

Her   You're right, that's cringe. Okay, fine. So, imagine I'm a stethoscope and I'm looking up inside you, the coldness is shocking and deep and I'm a mirror bouncing light right through you – there's no crevice or fold of you I can't see

Him   No.

Her   No?

Him   No.

Do you want to talk about it?

Her   It's impossible.

Him   I love you.

Her   No way.

Him   I'm – Sorry?

Her   I don't mean – Just not now. I can't think about that, as well as thinking about this.

Him   Have you done this before?

Her   No. But – my sister. She took the abortion pill and I stayed with her for the weekend. And it was a lot and uncomfortable and a bit sad, but it was okay.

Him   I'll stay with you.

Her   You don't have to. This doesn't have to be a big deal.

Him   Are you sure?

Her   No. It might be a really big deal, I don't know yet.

A long pause. Maybe the longest in the play so far.

Her   Before we found out about this, we didn't even know if we wanted to be together. And we don't really want a baby. We just want something to make everything else make sense. And that's not fair.

And even if we did want to be together. There's my career and your career and the fact we can barely take care of ourselves, and the fact I still want to drink and take drugs and you've got your Hinge and Tinder and Feeld.

Him   Yeah. And maybe I'll want to be with a man.

Her   Me too.

Him   That's unkind.

We don't have to be unkind.

Her   You're right. I'm sorry.

Him   I'll be with you during. Of course I'll stay with you.

Scene Nineteen. In Which It Ends, But Is Maybe Beginning

He sits nervously. Sounds of throwing up. She comes back in, looking grim, but trying to be cheerful. He maybe gives her something to drink through a straw.

Her   What's the most in love you've ever been?

Him   Seriously?

Her   No. I do think that's kind of funny of me, though.

Him   How are you feeling?

Her   Okay. Grim, but okay.

Him   How much blood?

Her   Carnage. You don't have to stay the night you know.

Him   Do you know what I'd really like right now?

Her   Please don't say sex.

Him   I'd like to lie together and spoon you and for you not to feel like you have to say anything.

Her   I'd like that too.

They lie together, snuggling into each other, both held.

Him   I want to say something that is really hard for me to say.

Her   Yes.

Him   I think we're making the right decision.

Her   Well, it'd be too fucking late for you to say anything else now.

Him   But also, I want you to know, that you've changed things for me.

Her   Really?

Him   And I don't mean in small ways, I mean in big big ways, something has changed.

Her   Do you think I've readied you for your next partner?

Him   What do you mean?

Her   Sometimes I feel like each relationship chips away at me a little more, but I give my partner a glow up. Like I'm an appetiser, and they they get to the main. I teach them things, new things about how to be better – that they then bring to their new relationship.

A pause.

Him   I guess that is kind of what I mean.

A watery sob.

Him   Not that I'm looking for anyone else. Or want anyone else. I'm not – I don't.

Her   I might need to throw up again.

It happened too soon. We wouldn't have been ready.

Him   No.

Her   We're not . . .

Him   Ready.

Her   To have a baby or look after the baby or change its nappy or stop it from rolling off tables or putting its fingers in sockets.

Him   But we could have lain in a bath together with it.

Her   Yes, we could have done that.

Him   It's not very safe, but we could have done that.

Her   After this, I don't know if I'll want to see you anymore, is that okay?

Him   Yeah.

Her   I was hoping you wouldn't say that, that was kind of a test.

Him   I don't think that's very healthy.

You're beautiful.

Her   Why do you say that?

Him   Because you're looking at me like you've forgotten.

Her   I didn't want anyone to feel pain.

Him   I didn't.

Her   That's disappointing too.

I am – sad.

Him   Me too.

Her   Do you know what about?

Him   It feels like we're saying goodbye to something.

Her   We had something. Even if it wasn't – not everything, even if – I think it's hoping.

Him   But we can still hope

Her   We can maybe.

Him   Maybe we can be. Maybe it's another time thing.

Her   Or another place thing.

Him   Maybe we can be friends.

Her   I'd like that.

Him   And there's a world too where – if you don't want to see me anymore, that's okay. But there's a world where if I want to have a baby in five years' time and you want to have one too, and the world isn't over. If we've both grown up a bit, can I call you?

For a complete listing of
Methuen Drama titles, visit:
www.bloomsbury.com/drama

Follow us on Twitter and keep up to date
with our news and publications
@MethuenDrama